MW01291774

feast of flowers

AVA.

ISBN-10: 1986680878
ISBN-13: 978-1986680875

for you

who never gives up.

for be hang ♥

♥

ᴧᴠᴧ.

*i still don't know what's good for me
after all these years.*

what are the lessons
that have taken you
the longest to learn?

forgiveness.
patience.
presence.
courage.
joy.
gratitude.

and always
love.

i know love is a very real thing.

it was here,
standing inside my door,
holding my hand
in the tenderest way.

i wanted everything to be intense.
my joy and my pain.

i wanted to know what it would feel like
if the sky were being ripped from the earth
and if the ocean could swallow the world.

are you depressed?

       i don't understand the question.

are you... sad all the time?

       am i? i didn't realize i was.
       i don't know.
       am i sad or is this just normal?
       i don't think i know the difference.

the hope will never leave you
and this is how it causes you pain.

i survived by
keeping my mouth above the water.

this is how i always survived—
        exhausted and gasping for air.

send love.
send for more love.

don't stop.

i just want to fall in love every night
and begin again in the morning.

waking up to find
your heart already breaking
feels like the whole day's over
before it's even begun.

how are people coping
inside of themselves?

what is keeping them together?
what is holding them up?

believing things will change
is the only thing keeping me going.

this heart
this constant breaking
over flowing
over giving of love.

i don't know how much is too much.
i don't know how to make it stop.

all i know is i will love
and love and love
and go on loving
until the loving is enough.

i don't want to wake up
unless it's in somewhere new.

somewhere
where i won't resent the sun
for existing so easily.

i just want to hear myself
above all the noise.

push my head up through the clouds
and just breathe.

close my eyes
and feel the sun on my face.

feel the blue sky
free alive
above me.

give me my delusions,
my impossible wants,
my jewels of grandeur.

i cannot live this small
and terrifying life.
i want big and i want open.

i want all the large spaces
and the most beautiful freedom.

i am demanding
and i am demanding
the foreverandever peace.

a tall drink of love in the afternoon.
a small kiss of courage every morning.

this hope,
this mad little thing—
   how it holds me up
   and keeps me standing
   over the cuts
   instead of falling in.

i fall in love
alone.

always alone.

i made myself pretty for you.
i made my body want for you.
wet for you.
give for you.

give
and give
and give for you

until there was nothing left
of me.

i was lonely
so i took off my clothes.

i stood in front of you
and felt more alone.

i am standing here—
   a feast before your eyes.
and still
you do not see me.

i never know how much of myself to give,
so i fall in love and i give everything.

i give
and give
and give
until the giving is smothering.

i love
i love so deeply
i am blind with love.

i get so lonely
i believe every word you say
how you love me
how you'll stay.

      i am so lonely
      i cling to pretty words.
      they always leave
      and i never learn.

it's just a flesh wound.
  it will heal.

this is what i tell my heart
when you leave me.

i couldn't have you
so i didn't want myself.

i punish myself always
in this way.

i let my worth be something
only someone else can give.

i let my love always be the one
with all the fault.

i don't love you in a way you understand
and i think the fault is in my love.

i'm not alone, i said.

> *i'm not alone.*
> *i have my loneliness*
> *and it will never leave me.*

remember the stillness inside you
when all decides to rot and ruin.

honor the silence in you
that wants only
of your peace.

have a good cry.
let it cleanse you.

let it bring you one step closer
  to understanding.

let it bring you one step closer
  to moving forward.

i want sex that means more than sex.

i want to know what that feels like—
to be close to them
and to know them intimately
without hating myself afterwards.
without giving myself away
to names, i won't remember.
to nights, i won't have to crawl out of.

i want to be held by someone
who holds me close to them
without having to hide
the hushed up parts of me.

i want that sex.
the sex that is comfortable and familiar
and with someone you feel safe with
and with someone you feel loved.

i always wanted it to hurt a little.
this has always been my problem.

i didn't know how to accept a love
that was full or complete.
i didn't know how to accept the love
that was real.

give me a love that was small or broken—
something i'd believe i could fix.
give me a love full of insecurity
and i'd drown myself inside of it.

i'm starting to learn that love is not
small or incomplete or broken.
love is something whole and beautiful,
magical and real.

love is not something
you need to mend or heal,
but it is something you work at and work for
every hour of every day,
and this difference can be hard to tell.

it is something that fills you,
not something you need to fill.

it is not love.
it is control in the name of love.

love is liberation.
love is breathing.
love is free.

go.
i am prepared.
i do not need you.

i will build a cocoon
with this pain,
   and you will go
   and i will change.

maybe all my loneliness
comes from not being understood.
maybe i've just grown too comfortable
in my own space.

i am different. i am not from here
and i do not belong.

but maybe i am here for a purpose.

maybe the only purpose is to love.

give love to the things that leave you too.

because though they're not for you,
it's still a way to carry more love
into the world

and love into the world is never wasted.

one day
you will love the way
you always wanted to love
and it will be glorious.

in the thick of my depression
i've learned i have to find
something else to live for
until i am finally okay enough
to live for myself again.

the pills are wearing off
and i'm starting to feel again.

you are telling me
you love me
and i'm beginning
to hear you.

like words under water
slowly coming up for air.

i do things now to keep the sadness
at least an arm's length away.
i take a long bath.
i remember to eat.
i text a friend. i tell them:
i'm sad but i'm okay.
little things, here and there,
to keep myself on a schedule.

i try to practice gratitude.
i go outside.
i tell the sun:
you are too bright, but i love you anyway.
i put on a song. i tell my mom:
i'm sorry.
and i pray.

i do a little more than i did yesterday.

i do and do and do
and hope that it's enough
and hope i'll be okay.

every time you think
the world is better off without you,
i go to kiss your forehead.

i cradle your head so gently in my lap
and remind you:
you are so bright. i only see the sun.

when you feel you can't
i lift your chin and raise your eyes
against the dark of the night
and you start to see:

you are made of stars full of hope
and you are just beginning.

forgive yourself for every failure
because you tried.

you tried so hard, love
and it's enough.

i am a collection of
all the people who love me
and i am a collection of
all the people who don't.

i am everything i ever will be
and i am everything i won't.

i am my past
and i am my future.

all i own is now.

i am who i am
as best as i can be.

i am who i am
who i am now.

now
you found me
and now
you want to know
who i am.

for that
you must stay.

it took years
for me
to know me
for me
to want me
for me
to love me.

it will take you the same.

i start every day fighting
or at least that's how it feels.

i fight to keep my heart soft.
to keep it open.
to make sure it feels full and is feeling.

then i shut my eyes. i sleep.
i sleep and i start again.

the hope is small
but it is everything.

some days
i don't believe the words i write.

some days
i want to burrow a hole into this bed
and never leave.

i think you know what i mean.

i know there is more to life than my pain.
i know there is love even when
i cannot feel it.

i live and die inside such small little hopes.
i live and breathe and blow hope
into my dreams.

i blow a kiss at night so
the moon will remember it's me.

i'm still here.

i'm still here
even if it's just barely.

i know what happiness is.
i am trying to write it next to me.

to bring it here to my lips
like water like wine.

the magic brewing in my mouth.
the power of calling it by its first name
and soon i will not have to wait.

soon i will be happy.

i see you.
i see you as you are.

you are so brave and so beautiful
    the way you stand there.
    the way you hold yourself up.
    the way you let yourself be.

your love of your existence is so powerful
a thousand revolutions are born
every time you breathe.

i've made up my mind.

i will carve out my sadness with a knife
like it's a tumor.

i will cut out a hole so big inside me that
every ray of light will burn right through
and you will mistake me for the sun.

i break into diamonds.
i fall like stars.
i turn
   and turn again.

i am hope in the dark.
i am love that cannot die.

i am power
and i am light.

i am.
i am.
i am.

my solitude, a wilderness.
a wildness, a refuge.

the peace i own on my own.

the unfettered heart. the love of being.
the songbird's song of freedom.
the crystal diamond dust of my soul.

when someone is brave enough
to ask you for the truth,
be kind enough to tell them.

what do you want to know?
i am not afraid.
i'll tell you everything.

i didn't want it to be like this.

where the truth comes out
and we stop talking to each other.

i wanted the truth to bring us closer.
to heal us.
not tear us apart.

the way some words
        stay with you
        and stay hurting you

all through your years.

i am interested in the things you survived.
the things that haunt you.

the things that have made you who you are
and make me love you.

none of these things could frighten me.

none of these things
could ever pull me away from you.

sometimes i catch you,

before you go off somewhere far
inside your mind.

i love you.
i need you to remember that.
i know you forget sometimes.

all those little places you go to,
thinking i can't go there,
thinking you're alone,

know that i am there with you
i am with you always.

in all the places you feel unloved.

i used to hide under water
and hold my breath
for as long as i could.

it was where i used to go
when i wanted to be alone,
it was where i could go and believe
just for a moment
the earth won't shake
and the people won't just die.

somehow,
you always knew where
you could find me.

you'd meet me
just below the surface
and show me just how easy it was
to come up for air.

i have been leaving myself
alone with myself
for far too long.

i don't know who i am anymore.

i have strayed
and i have frayed
far and away——

away from the edges;
i need to return home.

return to the home
inside of me
inside before i wrecked myself
and filled myself with
not love.

i need to return
to the kind and gentle lover.
the light. the forgiver.

the eye in my heart.

tell me how reckless you were
with your love.

tell me how deep the cut.
how long the wound.

tell me how,
with your hand on the blade,
you cut
and you tore
yourself apart.

then tell me
how you held yourself up.
how well you still loved
after you scarred your heart.

tell me the night
you stood and said:
i will love
and still love
and love myself again and again
and more and more.

i haven't quite learned how to forgive
so i spend most of my time alone.

my healing
still moving away from me.

my love
still hurting from the love
that is never returned.

you loved with your whole heart
and they left anyway.
and there is no shame in that.

there is no shame in
how deep and how far
you will go for love.

there is no shame in how
you let yourself break.

and when you let love be the one
that saves you in the end,
there is no shame in that either.

there is poetry in symmetry.

how beautiful and brave you are
for letting yourself die
for letting yourself live
for letting yourself rise

again
and again
and again.

i am learning
that when love wants to stay
it will stay.

and i am learning
that when love wants to go
it will go.

my superpower is
i feel everything
and i let it rip me apart every night
and still
i don't die.

instead,
i grow more open
and make more room.

all the good things in your life—

stack them
   one on top of the other
   and keep moving.
   keep glowing.

.

sometimes
knowing who you are
and knowing what you are capable of
can be the most freeing

loneliest thing in the world.

you wanted more god.
more meaning.

you wanted to rip this thread from your life
and stare straight into its eyes.

i am here, you say.

i am here
and i want to be here.
what more do you want from me?

don't you understand?
i write of happy things
because i am sad.

how very broken—
how very lost—
how very important it all was.
these formative years.
these trying times.

how else was i going to find myself?

how else would i know i could survive
my deepest darkest demons?

be relentless
in your pursuit for life.

be kind to yourself
when what you find
isn't what you wanted.

forgive yourself
and start again.

today i am grateful for this body.

how it still carries me after everything
i put it through.

this is the love i've been looking for
and it's been here inside me all along.

i will not soften myself
or make myself smaller.
i will not try to fit in spaces
that are not meant for me.

i will finally let myself be.

today you woke up,
looked at yourself in the mirror
and said:
  i am a beautiful revolution.
  i am alive
    and i love myself
    and i can begin again.

this is how you glow:

in the morning, you eat spoonfuls of sun
and you let the warmth gather
at the center of you.

you let it hold you down.
keep you close to earth

at an intimate distance.

you go and you fill yourself up
with so much light.
you shine so bright.
you shimmer. you rise.

you lovely, glowing human you.

because i am my mother's daughter
   i can do anything.

my mother's strength and power lives in me.

this morning
i promised devotion
to the womxn i wanted to be.

so i gave it.

and i give and give and give
until i am.

set boundaries.

remember there are other aspects of your life
that require your attention and care.

remember yourself as a priority too.

i am restless.
i move and i am moving.
i am leaving my heart
and i am looking out the window.

i memorize every face
i leave behind.

you are surrounded by everything beautiful

and yet,
you want more.

no one else can make you believe
you are deserving of love.

you need to believe in it for yourself.

can we put the world back together?

you asked me this this morning
  under the bright blue sky.
your face facing the sun
  your almond diamond eyes.

i looked at you and told you

  we will.

  little by little
    we will.

i'm still struggling to find the words. i don't understand why some things are the way they are. i have to believe we can always do something. i have to believe even the darkest of hearts can change.

i have to believe that we are not going to give up or give in to the fear that blinds us from our infinite capacity to love, that we will move beyond everything that divides us and we will move together, closer towards compassion and peace.

i am dreaming of a world where we can love and let love. be and let be.

it is too easy to hate. it is too easy to fear.
too easy to obey the invisible hand
and the voice that whispers
all those horrible things in your ear.

it is too easy to live in the hurt.
to wallow in it.
to bake a cake of sorrow
and close your eyes
and live beneath it.

i don't want to be those things.

let me be all the hard things.
let me love and love freely.
let me give until there's nothing left to give.
let me rise above
and find the joy beneath the hurt.
let me rise and should i fall,
let me rise again.
let these be the things that define me.

let me be defined by
the love and the hope and the peace
i never stop fighting for.

sometimes i do not choose healing.
sometimes i choose pain and anger
over and over
until i learn.

but i do learn.

i want to heal.
put it in the water.
let it listen to the moon.
let it wash over me in waves.

i return to water
and water remembers me,
embraces me in the only way
water knows how
with attention,
asks me:

how is your heart?
are you sleeping well?
why are you still not at ease?

water reaches
and holds my hands
and covers them clean
nourishes the skin
and reminds me:

we survive this life by loving deeply.

come honey. come lemon.
spread it over the night's black.
weave it in between the stars.
bathe yourself in moonlight
and rest.

it's going to take
as long as it takes.

everything in its right time.
everything in its right place.

i bathe the day from my skin
and sink into moonlight.
feed my body stars.
pour light into the cuts.
pour milk and honey.

i glow
into the dark.

i river
i wild

i move and
love me back
to all i used to be.

how hard it is
to stay soft and loving
in a burning world—

but i will keep my resolve
and i will keep my flowers.

our only purpose is to love.
to love ourselves and each other.
and if we don't know how, we learn.

that is all that is ever required of us
on this earth.

i drew strength from the river
and fell in love with the sea.

a flower does not cry
when you do not notice it.
its worth was never dependent
on your attention.

it is beautiful whether you see it or not.

there are always flowers before the fruit
my mama tells me.

my mama tells me
when you know, you know.

always be good to people
always be good to people
always be good to people

because life is so fucking hard.

you tell me
you are broken,
but i see you
for all that you are
and you're so fucking phenomenal
that even the sky falls to its knees
when you wake.

stop.
you don't have to fight here.

here you can be all the things you are
without fear.

love and *seen*—
please take these four letter words with you
and keep them safe.

and believe.

i will stand with you
until you can stand on your own.

some day you will be touched the way
you always wanted to be touched
and it will be real.

i planted flowers in the garden
so you would be reminded of earth's beauty.
i planted it there
so others can see it too.

i planted love in you
so you can carry it with you always.
i planted it there,
so others can feel it too.

this is how i will be remembered
when i am no longer standing
when i am no longer here.

this is how i'll never leave you.
this is how we can stay together.
this is how i'll always be near.

most of us are just doing the best we can
and sometimes
we're just not very good at the things we do
but i still feel there is something
incredibly beautiful in that.

we all fumble through this life
in the most ungraceful of ways
and yet, every morning
we still wake up and try.

we still find ways to love each other
in spite of our faults.

we still find things to live for
in spite of it all.

today we have a moment to ourselves
and everything in this moment is ours.

this is where we start.

we start where anything's possible.

we start here
in the flowers
in the sun.

pay attention to the things
you pay attention to.

let your own joy and wonder
guide you through your life.

there is something
magical and addicting
about going somewhere,
being alone, and finding yourself
in parts of the world
you never knew existed,
finding parts of yourself
you never knew you would find.

if we wanted to
we could go.

there's nothing to stop us.
there's nothing here
that could ever get in our way.

everywhere i go
i keep falling in love with the trees
and wanting to stay
   just a little bit longer.

once you leave home, you can never be
completely at home again. you go out into
the world and fall in love in every new
beginning, and you end up leaving a piece of
you in every new place you find.

this is why you always feel like you're
missing something.

you have been leaving whole pieces of your
heart all over this world, pieces of you that
can never return to you the same.

this is the beauty and the pain of loving
the way that you do. this is your one
remarkable life—
never whole, but always full.

you are wild and reckless,
full of adventure.

you love and love and love
and you love to no end.

to travel alone
is a gift for the mind.

the quiet.
the freedom of thought.

the infinite conversations
between me and my soul.

to wander the streets
of a city unknown.

no binds.
no ties.

an adventure of growth.

there are no limits to where i will go.

i can never stay in one place for too long.
i'd go mad if i knew what
to expect everyday.

i find comfort in the leaving
and all the new things.
new loves. new hurts.

let me feel too much. let me die from it.
let me never be too comfortable in this skin.

i was never born to be found.
i was always born to be free.

i want to do more than just live.

i want to feel.
i want to love.
i want to give.

and i want it all to consume me.

keep following your heart.

it won't always be easy,
but it'll be the most important thing
you do.

o sweet adventure,
please last forever
and keep my heart wild too.

your heart,
the feast of flowers
   full of hope
   full of dreams

may you always
bloom so boldly

so madly
in the sun.

AVA. currently lives in southern california and she wants you to know you are incredible and you are loved with a love far beyond this earth.

contact her at vav-ava.com

Made in the USA
San Bernardino, CA
28 April 2018